Once Upon a Time A Little Eaglet Named E9

By Liz Grindstaff

ISBN-13:
978-1729625507

ISBN-10:
1729625509

Acknowledgment

I would like to thank

Kathy Kochanowski for letting me use her picture.

Also Desiree Deliz for taking my picture that

is on the back cover of the book .

Dick Pritchett and North Fort Myers Church of Nazarene

for allowing the photographers and camera fans on their property .

Disclaimer

My intent for this book is to create a memory and this is my experience and my opinion .

Dedication

I would like to dedicate this book to all my friends that joins me day in and day out to observed precious Raptors.

Deborah Howell

Bill Serr

Karen Reynolds

Jan Woods

Jessica Ridgle

Diana McCunne

Jeanne (raptor fan)

Pam Meyers

Dee Kelly

Jeffery Jansen

Donna Lee

Alice Lukasik

Christine Mudd Caro

Kathy Kochanowski

Desiree Deliz

Barb Henry

Debbie Guadagnino

Marco Rose

Lisa Yttri

Lorelei Hanson

Kathy Bierman Haddon

Debi DuLaney Myers

Marti Lord

Marie Lapointe-Chim

Dave Eppley and Kaylee

Ted Waldron

Dave Chandler

Vickie O.

Robert Steagall

Dave Mintz

Robert Kimbrell

Jay Quintero

Chris Damerow

Roberto Darling

Among others that I may forget to mention .

In loving Memory of

Fran Bennets

Cathey Reams

Monika Wilson

Paul Wyman Henry Sr

Tom

and among others that left us too soon .

As I was ready to print my book I just learn the sudden pass of our friend Jeffery Jansen a great person, he will be missed dearly every morning at SWFL nest and his stories of the beloved Eagle family. Soar high and say hi to Ozzie and others .

The dedication and the
Love of wildlife is amazing.
Brings joy to everyone who captures
every moment and make great memories
that will last forever.

Introduction

A Little Eaglet came to the world
On December 31st at 7:33am
Little did we know it became famous.
As everyone watch from cams
and fall in love with the only One Eaglet
E9 at SWFL nest and many of
Eagle watchers have   nick names for E9;
some call Niner , Peepers , Prince and
among other nick name E9 got .
As the all world watch on how
the story unfold into everyone's eyes
and steal everyone's heart .
Here is A little story of E9 so I remember....

So it begins.......

So it begins

Once upon a time

An Eaglet born at SWFL

on December 31st at 7:33am

Everyone watch hatch and cute little bobblehead
came to the world .

As I await for E9 to take the first peek

from the rails .

How can you not fall in love .

Harriet and E9

Another one Harriet and E9

Harriet and E9 watching

I would love to know what they are thinking

I know Humans can put words right !! (laughing)

Dads turns with E9

M15 (Dad) and E9 both watching everything that is flying by

Closer look of M15 (Dad) and E9

Have to love this one kinda like a kiss

of course Human thinking (laughing out loud)

E9 wingersicing

Time is flying.... E9 is now wingersicing to get the strength needed .

Hello World

E9 looking

and everyone on the ground is watching

as many pictures has being taking.

If E9 only knew ...

E9 is getting bigger little by little

As days pass by E9 is growing

Here is Harriet and E9

A little Story of the air plant and E9

A little Story of the air plant and E9

On February 4 Harriet brought in

an air plant for the nest, then

 E9 got curious about what was that.

I have to tell you that

was the most memorable moment

as we all watch .

E9 grab the air plant

 and the look of Harriet, was priceless

as I can hear all photographers

with the sound of the camera shutters

capturing that moment that make us

all laugh .

Here comes Harriet with air plant

E9 and air plant

E9 " Hey Ma what am I supposed to do with this "
"Is this is a new toy for me "

Harriet s face

And someone came up with an idea to imitate E9

Kathy make us laugh that day like no other
and I have to thank you for that .

I will always remember... who wouldn't (lol)

E9 getting bigger

E9 sweet face

E9 watch as M15 (Dad) brings food

E9 getting a lift getting ready for fledge

E9 keep wingersicing hey "I am ready"

Fledge Day

Fledge Day

The moment arrived and

E9 accidentally fledge March 14 at 7:22am

As I arrived at the nest

I saw E9 flew beautifully

to the West pasture

like was ready to go.

Sometimes I wonder if E9 meant to do it .

Only E9 knows.

Everyone watching worried about it ;

as millions of heart beating so hard

and E9 was having a good time, playing

with horse poo (laughing out loud).

E9 flew a little further then back

and to the fence .

While E9 was perched at the fence watching

the new world, new adventure already start

and to go back to the nest it is the question;

but who wants to go back if you are having

so much fun , something new and a lot to
explore.

E9 was having a blast of the lifetime.

While millions were worry about it .

E9 :

"Hey I am at the west Pasture , love this new ground world"

E9 at the fence

E9 watching M15

M15 (Dad) delivering fish and E9 watch

E9 goes to the ground to claim the fish

that M15 (Dad) deliver.

Then... here comes Harriet

E9 was back and forward was not

interest in eating wants to explore the area .

Gets little piece of the fish then back out
and walk the road .

Then take off to the pasture ,

since a car was coming and Harriet and
M15 also take off to the pasture.

Then E9 came back under the fence and
start walking like own the place .

Was fun watching E9 like a boss (laughing
out loud).

Another memorable moment .

E9 went under the fence and....

Here comes E9 walking down the road

After that walk under the fence to the west pasture and flew to the tree and spend the night there.

The next day E9 return to the nest and now everyone can relax.

E9 beauty

I can open my eyes and see

your beauty.

M15 (Dad) deliver food

E9 and Harriet watching M15 leave

M15 Delivering fish to E9

M15 landed on the snag tree while E9
squeee

The story of the fish that went overboard

Once upon a time M15 flew to the nest with a fish and the fish went overboard .

As both E9 and M15 watch and look down...

E9 to M15 : " Dad that was my fish "

M15 to E9 : "Yep, you have to go get it other wise your mom will "

E9: " but Dad".....

Harriet saw what happened and flew to

the ground and she yield

Harriet : " Hey did you all lost something"

(of course I am laughing out loud putting words
on this picture after all is my human thinking)

Harriet took off to the tree and

E9 flew and try to claim the fish

E9: "Ma it is my fish "

Harriet: " Oh yeah so you think"

Harriet take off with the fish

Harriet to E9 : " catch me if you can "

Harriet on the ground and E9 arrived

and joined Harriet and E9 claimed

the fish now.

Lesson will begin

as the parent will show E9

skills needed for survival.

M15 (Dad) just arrived and Harriet and

E9 watch him landing .

Harriet and M15 (Dad) watching closely

at E9 eating the fish.

Hint :better eat it quickly or someone will

steal it from you.

Always protect your prey.

Here is M15 (Dad) working his

left talon and getting closer for the steal .

Lesson for E9

M15 (Dad) steal the fish from E9 but

wait... not too fast Mr (lol)

Harriet got him now

let the battle begin .

Now Harriet is getting the fish from M15 (Dad) while E9 watch.

Harriet has the fish now

E9 got close to Harriet to get the fish,

maybe will get fed by Harriet so is

what E9 think , (or my human thinking)

while M15 (Dad) watch .

Wrong ...

Harriet says no get your own fish.

This behavior is normal, it is needed

for survival since E9 is the only

Eaglet and parents are teaching E9 to be

more aggressive.

After all E9 got M15 (Dad) left talon swing lol

and got a piece of the fish

was great to see this .

How Harriet and M15 (Dad) teaching E9

survival skills that will prepare him/her, in the

new world.

E9

"I got a piece"

Another great milestone is when E9 took

the fish to the nest.

That was great to see .

E9 arrived with the fish to the nest

great job !!!

Another great milestone .

E9 at yonder pond and taking the first bath,

I was happy to see it. An experience that I will
remember forever is... that I learned how to
record a video despite the lighting wasn't
great that day .

E9 has being learning to maneuver as well, when crows bombarding in a fly.

Watching that is like they where dancing

in the sky .

More lessons for E9 .

When E9 came back from Yonder pond, a

Sub Adult follow and landed at the snag tree

E9 yield and the other Eagle didn't care.

Was good too see another Eagle that is thriving as well. After that the Sub Adult take off.

E9 fly free

Tender Moments

E9 and M15 (Dad)

E9 love to play on that tree and goes upside down, so funny to watch.

Upside down E9 goes

E9 ready to take off, so beautiful

Love E9 when fly away then comes back

and also when goes to tree

E9 love to play a lot .

E9 landing

Another Landing ...

when E9 open wings it is magical.

E9
someone is watching me

E9

As I sitting here watching my home and to think

 I may leave soon to a new adventure

that awaits me.

The world is waiting as I sit here and

watch my home that soon I will leave ...

to do what Eagles do, and become

a magnificent one.

E9 glorious watching home

I wrote the following :

One last fly

One last fly
Is it E9?
It seems like yesterday you just hatched.
You make us laugh
And yes we worry...
    One last fly
Is it E9?
It seems that you just fledged accidentally
 and was beautiful your fly to the west pasture
    and to walk on the road like you own it,
      that makes us laugh.
One last fly
Is it E9?
The mantles , the squeeeeee
You have surprised us
You have learn from your parents
And you watch everything they do
    and you learn as you go.
You took your bath at yonder pond.
    Are you ready E9 one last fly
This is your time
Fly free
you will be amazing Eagle.
We are going to miss you E9
You imprint all the areas as well our hearts
One more fly.

E9

one last fly

It was also great to see E9 soaring
with M15 (Dad) and E9 was doing maneuvering
since was the only Eaglet, was amazing
to see that.

I smile it was so touchy and melt my heart
so I wrote the following:
Beneath my wings
I take you sweet baby,
Lets go to places
to hunt and fish.
Follow me and I will teach you
survivals skills you most conquer
and in due time will come to you
and your instinct will kick in …
Lets soar high
Beneath my wings lets soar high.

E9 and M15 (Dad) soaring together
Beneath my wings...

E9 and the moon

E9

Preening

I wonder where E9 get that from …

Harriet of course the Queen of preening.

As the season was getting closer
I know E9 has to leave and as
 I see the moon I merge 2 pictures
 into one that makes it perfect for what I
 wrote:
Love you to the moon and back
Now you will start your new journey
on your own.
New adventure awaits you
Fly high E9
I wish you the best
Love you to the moon and back .
You will be an amazing Eagle.
Yes we are going to miss you .
You maybe still around but not for long
Soar E9
Love you to the moon and back.

E9 Love you to the moon and back

Family
E9
M15
Harriet

Thanks for reading

I enjoy every minute, every moment of E9

and how this little Eaglet transform the all world into one .

Forgetting the noise and transporting

us all into something different .

Learn about raptors it is fascinating and

I have to say that cams has help a lot,

to see what they go through day by day

and help us to be a better human being

and understand more about wildlife, to be aware.

We see good the bad and the ugly,

but after all , some others are thriving .

When the season began; I just got my new camera and I didn't know how to use it that well .

Little by little I was getting use to it and learning more, as I really want to capture every moment .

Really special I have to say.

Every Season will bring you something different; all at Eagle time and we must remember that story can change.

I am happy that E9 made it through this

season and I hope will continue to do so and have the family and conquer the world .

Also I will never forget eggbert

only nature knows ….

I hope you all enjoy my little story .

E9 standing tall and proud

The little Story of E9

You will be missed .

E9 and Sun Kiss

46778614R00051

Made in the USA
Middletown, DE
31 May 2019